# The Final Farewell:
## Preparing for and Mourning
## the Loss of Your Pet

by Marty Tousley, RN and Katherine Heuerman

Our Pals Publishing Company
Phoenix, Arizona

**The Final Farewell —**
**Preparing for and Mourning the Loss of Your Pet**

ISBN 0-9657128-1-8

Our Pals Publishing Company
Phoenix, Arizona

Publisher's Cataloging-in-Publication
(Provided by Quality Books, Inc.)

Tousley, Marty.
    The final farewell : preparing for and mourning the loss of your pet / by Marty Tousley and Katherine Heuerman.
    p. cm.
    Includes index.
    ISBN: 0-9657128-1-8

       1. Pets—Death—Psychological aspects.
2. Pet owners—Psychology. 3. Bereavement—Psychological aspects. I. Heuerman, Katherine.
II. Title

SF411.47.T68 1997       155.9'37
                     QBI97-41211

# The Final Farewell:
## Preparing for and Mourning the Loss of Your Pet

## by Marty Tousley, RN and Katherine Heuerman

**Contents**

# Contents

## Let Me Go

When I come to the end of the road
And the sun has set for me,
I want no rites in a gloom-filled room.
Why cry for a soul set free?

Miss me a little — but not too long
And not with your head bowed low.
Remember the love that we once shared.
Miss me — but let me go.

For this is a journey that we all must take
And each must go alone.
It's all a part of the Master plan,
A step on the road to home.

When you are lonely and sick of heart,
Go to the friends we know
And bury your sorrows in doing good deeds.
Miss me — but let me go.

*Author Unknown*

# Foreword

Anyone who has ever experienced the unconditional love and special joy that an animal companion brings to his or her life knows all too well, or will come to know, the deep sadness and very real pain associated with having to say good-bye. Drawing from their professional expertise and heartfelt experiences of losing their own pets, authors Marty Tousley and Katherine Heuerman have created a thoughtful yet practical guide pet owners can turn to for comfort, advice, encouragement and support in preparing for the loss of a beloved companion. And, in understanding that the bond we share with our animal companions is not broken when they leave us, the authors provide the means for taking the first steps toward healing. For this, we acknowledge and thank them.

**Kenneth D. White**
*Executive Director*
**The Arizona Humane Society**

## Endorsements

Veterinarians are often called upon to help families come to grips with the mortality of their beloved pets. Faced all at once with making difficult decisions and final arrangements, they long for the kind of information and help that *The Final Farewell* provides.

Marty and Katherine have put together a frank but gentle guide to help all of us face the realities of losing a feathered, scaled or furred family member. By openly and honestly discussing the hard issues that most of us agonize over but few address, they help calm the fear of the unknown. And in a society that tends to regard animals as property, they legitimize our grief and allow us to mourn our animal friends.

This is a book that all members of a veterinary staff should read and absorb. They also should make it available to their clients, to help them at the time of their pets' final farewell.

Kate McCullough, D.V.M.
Glendale, Arizona

Having worked closely with pet bereavement throughout my 16 years as a veterinarian, and having experienced pet loss first-hand, I consider *The Final Farewell* to be the most comprehensive and informative book on pet loss I have reviewed. Sensitive issues that most adoring pet owners don't want to think about — or don't even realize they should think about — are thoroughly addressed, including options for care of the pet's body after death. The book also serves to explore and explain the deep emotions that emerge once the human-companion animal bond is broken. I highly recommend the book and commend the authors on a wonderful and helpful publication.

Jim Flegenheimer, D.V.M.
*Veterinary Consultant,* Pet Grief Support Service
Companion Animal Association of Arizona, Inc.

When we lose a beloved companion animal, we lose far more than a "pet." We also lose the uncomplicated, unconditional love that only an animal can give to us. The pain of our loss can be equal to the depth of the love that we shared. As one who's worked in pet bereavement for many years, I know all too well the confusion and turmoil people go through when faced with such a loss. Along with understanding and support, they need information they can use. *The Final Farewell* provides all of that. The most comprehensive book on pet loss and memorialization I've ever read, this is a guide that prepares us for the decisions we must make, supports us in our grieving and reminds us that, when each of us must say that final farewell, the love we shared with our dear animal friends will live forever.

Joyce D. Lemons
*President,* Companion Animal Association
of Arizona, Inc.

*Volunteer Coordinator,* Pet Grief Support Service

## Preface

From our separate experiences with pet loss in our personal lives, and in our different ways of working with grieving pet owners in our professional lives, we have come to know firsthand the issues and problems connected with loving, losing and remembering our special friends.

By the time we met as volunteers in a pet grief support service three years ago, we each had found our own way to work through our separate griefs and come to terms with the loss of our own pets seven years earlier. We discovered that we'd both been affected deeply enough by the deaths of our special pets to have redirected our careers into the field of pet bereavement. Each of us now works, in different contexts, with those who've suffered the loss of their beloved companion animals.

Our own experience has taught us that it is better to plan for the death of our pets as far in advance as we can. By pooling our knowledge and experience in pet loss and bereavement and the after-death care of companion animals, we hope to share with you what we have learned. This book is our effort to provide you with the direction, comfort and support you will need *in advance of your pet's death*, so that when the time comes, you will understand what options are available for the final disposition of your pet's body; so you can pre-plan what will happen to your pet's body after death; so you can make the most of the time you have left to experience and draw closure on the special relationship you have with your pet; and so that, in the end, you will understand your reactions, resolve your feelings of grief and come to terms with your loss.

We begin by sharing with you the details of our own individual experiences with pet loss.

## Marty's Story

He was supposed to belong to my oldest son, but from the beginning, the whole family knew better. He was the most adorable puppy I'd ever seen: a blonde powder puff with the face of a Teddy bear. His baby charm was something he'd never lose, for even when full grown, he remained a delightful puppy-mixture of poodle, cocker and little boy: intelligent, loving and strong, full of mischief, adventure and fun. His ears were set low and close to his head, and were covered with long, silky blonde hair. His expressive brown eyes were perfectly outlined in black, with eyelashes so dark and long they seemed to be tipped with mascara.

His tail was his barometer. Like a weather flag on a yacht, it told all there was to know about his mood. He would wait on the deck in the backyard for me to come home at night, precariously perched on the back of a bench, peering over the fence. At the sound of my car in the driveway, my husband would cheerfully announce, "The mother dog is home!"

At this he would wag his tail, then his entire hindquarters, usually with such exuberance that he would send himself flying off the deck in a heap, landing in the shrubbery.

When I'd sit visiting with a friend over coffee at the kitchen table and he felt left out, from under the table would come an insistent "thump, *thump*, THUMP!" of his tail against the floor, until all eyes were upon him. Then, narrowing his gaze and curling his lips into a silly, satisfied grin, he'd roll over on his back and offer his belly to be scratched.

His vocabulary rivaled any preschooler's, especially if the words had anything to do with eating. The surest way to bring him in an instant was not to call him by name, but to ask if he wanted a cookie. He loved "people" food, and was quite clever at gaining access to it. One Easter morning I discovered that every last one of the dozen colored eggs I'd placed in a crystal bowl in the center of my dining room table was gone. The chairs were pushed in; the tablecloth was undisturbed; the centerpiece was otherwise intact. But there *he* sat, grinning from ear to ear, "thump, *thump*, THUMPing" his tail against the floor. I would never have known he was the culprit, were it not for his whiskers and beard, now tinted in lovely pastel shades of purple, yellow and green.

He was my clown when I needed a laugh, but as my sons grew into adolescence (wanting and needing less of my attention and affection), and as my husband began to travel more in his work (leaving me alone three and four nights a week), he became my constant companion. He was my own little person — always eager for me to cuddle him, hug him, take him onto my lap or into my arms. Wherever I went, he was there. When I sat down to read he curled up on my footstool. When I lay on the sofa, he'd hop up and lie on my legs. As I worked at my desk in my office, he'd lie with his chin on my feet. He lay at my side when I tended my garden, and sunned himself by the pool while I basked on my raft in the water. When my husband was away on a business trip, he slept in my bed at night and kept me safe and warm. Without saying a word, I shared my deepest problems and sorrows with him, and he would always listen, loving me unconditionally and accepting me as I was, without judgment or reproach.

But there was a part of him I knew I'd never own. He loved to hunt rabbits, and he would go through any obstacle on earth to chase them. Our two-acre yard was surrounded by fence embedded in concrete eight inches beneath the ground. Despite all our best efforts, when he wanted out, there was no stopping him. He'd spend days excavating a tunnel, just a few inches each day, in those stolen moments when no one was watching him. He'd wait until the coast was clear — then he'd be off. He'd be gone for hours, sometimes past sunset, finally appearing at the patio doors like some pathetic stray: ears matted with burrs, stuck into themselves at crazy angles atop his head; eyes bloodshot, lids drooping; paw pads cut and bleeding; body and tail covered with tics and briars and mud. One of the family would always be stationed there, ready to receive him. Tenderly he'd be delivered to the laundry tub in the basement, where I'd set about the long and arduous task of cleaning him up. I'd hold his weary head in my two hands, so grateful that he was home and safe, yet so angry at him for leaving us again — for causing me so much work — for putting himself through the agony that lay ahead for both of us, as one by one I pulled hundreds of tics and thorns from his bruised and bleeding flesh.

"Was it worth it?" I'd ask — but all I had to do was look into his hunter's eyes, and hear the "thump, *thump*, THUMP!" of his tail which said, of course, "You *bet!*"

One Christmas Eve he went off hunting and was gone for four days. It was the saddest and most painful holiday I had ever known. I was inconsolable. How does one resolve that kind of grief? Was he dead? Was he hurt and lying in some cold, dark ditch somewhere? Had someone picked him up and stolen him? Would I ever find out what had happened to him? How could I go on with celebrations with family and friends when my heart was breaking? Shouldn't we search for him one more time? How could I be so upset over a *dog*?

But, wonder of wonders, he did come home. A lovely grandmother had found him and taken him in. Although he'd lost his collar and tags, when her grandson visited and saw him three days later, he recognized him as our dog. When the phone call came, I was overcome with joy. In an instant, it had become the happiest and most wonderful Christmas of all.

Eventually, of course, his luck ran out. The day finally came when he would escape from the yard for the very last time. Chasing yet another rabbit across yet another highway, he was hit by a car. Someone found him in the ditch by the side of the road, checked his collar and tags, and telephoned the tragic news to us. My son picked him up, saw that he was seriously injured, and took him immediately to our veterinarian. X-rays confirmed that his back was broken, his spinal cord severed. He couldn't stand; he had no bowel or bladder control. There was no saving him. After making the unbearably painful decision to euthanize him, our entire family gathered in the treatment room, holding him and each other as he was injected. He died quietly in my arms. The vet asked me what we wanted to do with his body. I had no idea what I wanted to do with his body — I wasn't even ready to think of my dog as *dead*, much less as a *body*! Not knowing what else to do, we wrapped him in a blanket and took him home.

I held him for hours afterward, rocking him, petting him, memorizing his Teddy-bear face, crying and saying good-bye. Finally we buried him in the backyard, underneath some lilac trees, and marked his grave with a wooden plaque my husband carved as a tribute to his memory.

I was totally unprepared for this — not only for my dog's death and what to do with his remains afterward, but also for the intensity of my reaction. It wasn't as if I was unfamiliar with grief. By that point in my life I'd already lost to death a newborn infant, my father, my mother-in-law, a sister-in-law and several close friends. Having had a wide variety of pets throughout my life, I'd already loved and lost a significant number of them as well. In my private practice as a therapist I had been studying death and dying and had been specializing in bereavement counseling for many years. Both my experience and my training had taught me that death comes to all living creatures. I certainly knew that nothing lasts forever. But losing *this* little dog was different. I loved him like no other animal I had ever known, and when he died I was absolutely devastated. My grief was as strong as any I had ever felt before. I canceled long-made plans to return to my home town for my high school class reunion, telling those who were expecting me that I'd had a death in the family.

My strong reaction to my dog's death made me realize that the loss of a beloved pet is a loss that needs to be comforted, too. I began to investigate the nature of people's attachment to their pets, reading all I could find about the human-animal bond and learning as much as I could about people's reactions to the loss of their companion animals. Eventually I discovered the pet bereavement movement, whose focus is on understanding and respecting the person's level of attachment to the pet, the role the animal played in the person's life, and the significance of the loss *from the person's point of view.* I began to incorporate my newfound knowledge about pet loss and bereavement into my practice as a therapist. Today I still work primarily with people who are grieving the loss of their loved ones — animal as well as human.

As I look back on it now, I'm fairly comfortable with most of what we decided to do when my special dog died so suddenly that summer day so long ago. Nevertheless, in the ten years since his death, my husband and I have moved several times, and this dear little dog's grave is still in New Jersey, in a backyard that now belongs to someone else. Knowing what I know now, there are some things I would've done differently, if only I had been prepared, if only I had planned ahead, and if only I had known what all my options were.

## Katherine's Story

She was a clumsy but beautiful six-month-old Irish Setter when she joined us in 1971. She may not have been what I expected, but then I'm often surprised by what fate brings me.

She came with a very fancy name — Lady Campbell McDuff — but we just called her Duffy. Her former owner wanted to interview my husband and me to see if we met the ownership criteria he had set for this beauty. But once I saw her and felt her presence, I knew she would never leave our sight again — and she never did.

Since my husband worked out of town most of the time, Duffy and I became the best of friends. We loved late-night talks, going to drive-in movies together, playing softball games and, of course, any kind of road trip. Duffy became my confidante and protector.

Life continued this way for three years until Dan, my first child, was born. Something changed overnight: Duffy no longer was just my pal and protector. Now she was taking care of the *two* of us.

One summer day I put Dan in his playpen in the shade near the shed, so I could still hear him playing as I worked in the garden. Duffy was lying in the cool grass, sound asleep beside Dan's playpen. Suddenly from behind the shed I heard Duffy barking furiously. I rushed to the playpen to make certain Dan was safe, then ran around the corner, only to find the electric meter reader frozen in place as he faced our protective Duffy, who had planted herself firmly between the stranger and the playpen. She refused to let him move until I told her it was all right.

Three years later my sweet little Sarah was born. Now there were even more people for Duffy to protect, and lots more exciting action! She loved every moment, thriving on the activity, socialization and excitement of it all. As the years passed she insisted on including herself in all the children's activities, never wanting to be left out. At harvest time, she'd pull a wagon filled with Sarah and all the vegetables picked fresh from the garden, with Dan happily walking alongside. We'd end up at the housing development for the elderly, where the children would sell their vegetables for five or ten cents apiece. It may have been getting a little more crowded when we went to the drive-in movies, but we always had fun. Of course, Duffy and I were the only ones still awake for the second show!

Although she had some cancerous growths removed when she was six years old and again when she was 10, Duffy lived an otherwise healthy, happy life. By the time she was 15, I was divorced, and the four of us — Dan, Sarah, Duffy and I — ventured off to Phoenix, Arizona to begin a new life. Three months later, Duffy became suddenly and terribly ill.

It was December, just two weeks before Christmas, and my mother had come to spend the holidays with us. Duffy had been fine the night before, but around one o'clock in the morning she went into convulsions. I didn't know what to do. Not yet having developed a relationship with a veterinarian, I looked in the Yellow Pages and frantically began placing calls. After what seemed an eternity, I finally reached an all-night clinic. Leaving my children in my mother's care and fighting back tears, I rushed Duffy to the clinic. Afraid of what was coming next, I kept trying not to fall apart, all the while thinking of how long she had been with me and how much she meant to me.

Within two hours the X-ray results were in: the cancer had come back. There was a large mass in her chest area. Given her age and the size of the mass, the doctor said it was hopeless.

Duffy was not in pain, but she didn't respond to anyone, either. Clearly she was dying, and there was nothing I could do about it. After four hours I still couldn't make a decision about euthanasia. The clinic staff recommended that I go home and call them in the morning.

Of course I couldn't sleep — neither could I afford the luxury of not going to work that next day. When I called the clinic in the morning, I found out her condition hadn't changed. She wasn't responding to anything they tried to do for her. I would have done anything to save her, but I knew that realistically I didn't have the money and she didn't have a chance.

That day was one of the worst ones of my life. I finally accepted the fact that Duffy was leaving us, and I agreed to her euthanasia. But I didn't see how I could ever overcome the guilt, the pain and remorse I felt. And on top of all of that, the clinic staff was telling me I had to decide what I wanted to do with Duffy's body after she was dead! *Wait a minute*, I thought. I *just made the most difficult decision of my life, and you're asking me to make this one, too?*

I had contemplated sending Duffy's body back home to be buried on my parents' farm, but that was more costly than I could afford and I would rarely get to visit her grave that way. Eventually I decided to have her body cremated, but separately, so that her cremains could be returned to me.

One week passed with no return of Duffy's cremains. When another week went by, I called to ask what had happened to my dog. I was merely told that the facility was busy.

At the end of three weeks, when Duffy's cremains finally were returned to me, I was beside myself. I began asking questions, and the more I found out, the more upset I became.

When I asked why it had taken so long, the facility owner told me he was backed up and running behind. He just hadn't had time to get to my dog, he said. I snarled that obviously he needed to get extra help. When I asked to view the cremation facility, he told me it was not his policy to allow site inspections. Still not satisfied, I asked for the facility's address — and he was foolish enough to give it to me.

It took two more weeks for me to muster the courage to go to see it, without notifying the facility first. It was just as I had suspected: locked gate and totally surrounded by high walls. As I peered over the top of the wall, I didn't like what I saw inside. The place was filthy. There were bags of dead animals lying on the ground. These were people's pets, and no one was taking care of them properly! Since it was almost dark and no one was around, it was obvious that they would remain there at least until the next morning. Now, in addition to my grief over losing Duffy, I could picture how insensitively her body had been treated. There was also a very large doubt in my mind that the cremains that had been returned to me did, in fact, belong to her. I became determined that I'd do whatever I could to keep this outrage from happening to someone else.

Within six months I launched PALS ( Pet & Animal Lovers Service), which began as a part-time business out of my home. Although I worked another full-time job, my clients would wait for me until I was free in the evening to pick up their deceased pets. Working with a veterinary clinic that had cremation facilities, I would oversee and assist with the cremation of my clients' individual pets, making certain that the cremains were returned to the clients promptly, with all the dignity, respect, support and comfort I could offer them. Today, **PALS** is a full-time business whose services have expanded to include the pickup, transport, cremation, burial and preservation of companion animals throughout Arizona.

It was not until last year, as I was preparing a presentation on memorializing lost pets, that I realized how my entire business has itself become a memorial to my beloved Duffy. Her cremains rest in a container on the corner of my desk, where her presence is a constant in my daily work. All the samples of pet cemetery markers, cremation urns and other memorial products I display in my office have Duffy's name inscribed on them. When I work with clients who are grieving, or who are pre-planning what to expect, how to cope, what their options are and how much all of it will cost — I think back to how I felt when Duffy died, how frightened, unprepared and alone I was, not knowing what to do or whom to call. I try to give my clients the comfort and support I wish someone had given me when I lost Duffy.

After Duffy died, I wouldn't even consider getting another pet. I was fully prepared to grieve for her forever. I certainly didn't want to go through such a painful loss as this again. Three years went by, and in spite of my children begging me, we still had no pet in the house. I simply was not ready.

But then fate stepped in. One day as I visited a kennel with the pet products I was selling, a tri-colored Shetland Sheepdog came running up to me. We liked each other immediately and although I thought she was a love, I was not ready. The next week, when I had to return with another delivery, she spotted me instantly and ran across the yard to greet me. Her eyes were so inviting and her kisses so delicious! When I left that day, she left with me. I had been so certain that I'd never get another pet — but then I thought about what Duffy would've wanted. All she ever wanted was to please me, and she knew that this dear little dog would definitely please me! I never replaced Duffy — I just added another member to my family. Abigail Cromby (Abby, the princess) has been with me for several years now, and I still look back and wonder how I managed to live without this pal, this friend, this confidante.

My children are grown and on their own now. Once again it's just my wonderful dog and me. Abby is my dearest companion. Much as I don't want to think about her growing old and leaving me, I know it's inevitable. I suspect when that time comes, I won't hold up any better than I did with Duffy, but I know this for certain: I *do* know what to expect, what my options are, who will assist me, how the procedures will be handled, that the cremains I receive afterward will belong to Abby, and who will be there for my comfort and support.

## Introduction

Ordinarily we don't think about making final arrangements for our companion animals in advance, even though intellectually we know that their life spans are so much shorter than our own — and that fatal accidents and terminal illnesses can happen. In our death-denying culture, we have a hard enough time acknowledging our *own* mortality. Some of us may take care of our own funeral, burial or cremation arrangements well in advance of our deaths (or at least make our wishes known), but we rarely think to do so for our pets. Most people avoid such realities until they are forced to confront them.

When a pet is critically ill or has died, the mourning process and the decisions surrounding it are especially difficult. All at once owners must cope with overwhelming feelings of loss, make decisions, necessary arrangements for body care, and all too often deal with the insensitivity of others. Regardless of whether closeness to animals is accepted as normal in our culture, when faced with losing that special relationship, we're rarely prepared for the enormity of the grief that we feel. And until we're actually confronted with the situation, we may not realize that our pet's death carries with it the responsibility of arranging what will happen to our pet's body after death.

By understanding and accepting that losing our pets is inevitable, we have an opportunity to prepare before we suffer the shock of losing them. We need not wait until we're in crisis. From the authors' own experiences with pet loss and in our work with grieving pet owners, we know that the more you know what to expect, the more you know what your options are — and the more you can plan ahead — the less stressful the mourning process will be for you. It is our hope that this book will provide the information you need to prepare for and get through this most difficult time.

# Preparing for the Loss of Your Pet

**Anticipatory Grieving**

If your pet is aging, seriously injured or chronically or terminally ill, you may find yourself experiencing all the emotions of grief *in anticipation* of losing your pet. Grieving that begins *before* a death occurs is known as *anticipatory grieving*, and the physical and emotional reactions involved are the same as those experienced in normal grieving.

It is extremely difficult to watch your cherished pet's health and quality of life deteriorate over time. Constantly reminded that your pet's death is inevitable, you may experience intense feelings of guilt, denial, anxiety and ambivalence.

If expensive treatment or care is required, at times you may wish your pet would die — and then feel very guilty for having that wish. On the other hand, in an effort to cope with your feelings of guilt and loss, you may deny the seriousness of your pet's condition and, against all odds, spend time and money you can't afford to seek out more tests, more treatment and more surgery. If you're faced with the decision of euthanasia, you may be struggling with anxiety over separating from your pet, uncertain how you'll ever bring yourself to say good-bye. Torn between not wanting to see your pet suffer and not wanting to lose the animal, you may go to great lengths to postpone or to avoid the decision all together.

## Coming to a Decision

Deciding when and whether to euthanize your pet is probably one of the most difficult choices you'll ever have to make. But because your pet has just been diagnosed with a terminal illness may not be reason enough to resort to euthanasia. Depending on the stage and severity of your pet's illness or injury, and the resources you have available, you and your pet may still have many happy years left together. Exploring all aspects of the decision with your veterinarian and with others whom you trust is very important. Keep in mind, however, that in the end, the decision belongs to you and you alone.

If euthanasia is being considered for your pet, like most people you're probably wondering, "How will I know when it's time?" As you come to answer that question, here's what you might want to think about:

- What is your pet's general health and attitude? (Is your pet still happy with a zest for life? Miserable? In pain? Terminally ill? Critically injured with no hope of recovery?)

- What is the quality of your pet's life? (Is your pet still living with dignity?)

- How much care does your pet require?

- Can you afford the costs involved, in terms of time, money and emotional strain?

- What is your pet's prognosis? (Will more tests, treatments or surgery make your pet any better? Are there any negative side-effects from such tests or treatments?)

- How do you feel about euthanasia? (Do you

consider it an act of compassion?)

- Are there any signs from the pet that s/he is "ready to go"? (Some pets have a way of telling us these things.)

- Sometimes people keep their pets alive in order to meet their own needs (to not feel guilty, to not let go) rather than to meet the needs of the pet. Hard as it may be, ask yourself if this could be going on with you.

## Preparing for What Lies Ahead

Most of us find it very difficult to think about planning ahead for the death of our pets. We act as if merely thinking or talking about the pet's dying will somehow make it happen — or we act as if *not* thinking or talking about our pet's illness will somehow make it go away. Yet the reality is that none of us has the power to cause the death of another merely by thinking or talking about it — and illnesses aren't prevented or cured simply by choosing not to think about them.

Detaching from a cherished pet is just as difficult whether it happens suddenly or over an extended period of time. But having time to prepare for what lies ahead can be one of the more positive aspects of anticipatory grieving. You can make the most of the time remaining by talking with your veterinarian, family, friends and trusted others about the pet's death *as a probability* (not as a remote possibility). You can also use this time for:

- Feeling and expressing whatever grief feelings arise.

- Confronting and sorting out your own basic values and beliefs about death, dying and the afterlife.

- Thinking about and planning what to do with your pet's remains after death (keeping in mind what's best for your family and what's consistent with your own beliefs).

- Talking to your veterinarian to clear up any questions or reservations about your pet's diagnosis, treatment and prognosis. (Expressing your greatest fears enables both you and your veterinarian to plan out how to deal with them.)

- Thinking about and planning a ritual, ceremony or other way of memorializing your pet.

- Making your final days with your pet as special as possible and making treasured memories that will offer you comfort later (e.g. indulging in your pet's favorite activities; taking lots of pictures; taking a feather or clipping of fur; preserving a paw print).

- Taking care of *yourself* while caring for your sick animal (by getting enough nourishment, relaxation, rest and exercise).

## Exploring Questions About Euthanasia

There is probably no more difficult question than whether or not to euthanize a cherished companion animal. Yet when the quality of life for your pet has deteriorated, when your pet is suffering agonizing pain, or when costs of tests and treatments are prohibitive, euthanasia may be the most loving and humane choice for you and your pet.

As you come to this difficult decision, it's important to think through whatever questions you may have about the actual procedure, so you can discuss your concerns with your veterinarian. When the time comes, you'll be better prepared to use your own good judgment based on the reality of your particular situation.

Think about these questions, then arrange a time to discuss them with your veterinarian:

• How will the euthanasia be performed? (Usually the animal is injected with a tranquilizer, then an overdose of a sedative.)

• Where will the euthanasia be done? (Euthanasia can be done at your veterinarian's office or animal clinic, at your local Humane society or animal control facility, or at your own home. If your veterinarian doesn't provide at-home euthanasia, you can ask for a referral to one who does.)

• When will the euthanasia be done? (Try to schedule it at a time that's least traumatic for you, and when you can be accompanied by a friend or family member — especially if driving is involved.)

• Should my pet be euthanized immediately, or should the procedure be delayed? (It all depends upon the individuals involved. It may be easier to get it done while you are certain of the decision, since waiting for the inevitable may be difficult for you. Yet a planned delay can afford your family and your pet some time to make the most of your final days together.)

- What should I tell my child(ren)? (Children need the truth, in terms they can understand, with an opportunity to ask questions.)

- Should I/we be present during the procedure? (You know better than anyone what you feel capable of handling. You should be guided by what makes you feel comfortable and by what you think you can live with later. Some people consider being present as a final demonstration to the pet of their affection, and take comfort in knowing their pet is actually dead and at peace. Others prefer to remember their pet as it was, alive and active.)

- Will it matter to my pet if I'm present? (Pets feel more secure in the company of people they know, and pets do not have the same awareness of death or the anxiety before death that humans do. An owner's anxiety can be conveyed to both pet and veterinarian, but if the owner is calm, the pet will remain calm also.)

- What will I do with my pet's remains? (Be aware that you are responsible for arranging what will happen to your pet's body after death. Many options are available, including disposal, cremation, burial and preservation. It would be wise to discuss these options *in advance* of your pet's death, either with your veterinarian or with a representative from a pet cemetery or pet crematory.)

# Planning for the Death of Your Pet

**Why It's Wise to Plan Ahead**

Much as we don't like to think about it, death and loss are natural parts of living. Sooner or later our cherished pets will grow old, become seriously ill or sustain an injury that can't be fixed.

Because the life spans of most domestic animals are naturally shorter than our own, it is quite likely that at some point each of us will experience the death of a pet. Accepting that reality gives us a great deal of control over how we'll handle the situation when it arises, because we can choose to plan ahead for it. We don't have to wait until we're overwhelmed with grief to think about the practical aspects of pet death and body care, and how we could best preserve and honor our pet's memory thereafter.

Whenever an animal dies, *someone* must decide what to do with its remains. Although the responsibility for that decision rests with the pet's owner, oftentimes it is left to the veterinarian to make such arrangements. A distraught owner struggling to cope with the trauma of loss is not in the best position to ask intelligent questions and make an informed, well-thought out choice about body care. Although ethically obligated to answer all your questions, your veterinarian may not have the training, facilities or time to provide sensitive after-death pet care. And when the time comes, if you don't already know what questions to ask or what your preferences are, your pet's body may not be disposed of in a manner that's acceptable to you.

Using this book as a guide, we encourage you to think through what you want to do with your pet's remains while your pet is still young and healthy, *before* illness, injury or old age strikes.

Even if your pet's death is sudden and unexpected, be aware that you still can arrange to have your pet's body held in a refrigerated room or a freezer for a reasonable period of time, until you're better able to think clearly and decide what to do. Ask whether your veterinarian provides this service, or can refer you to someone who does.

We suggest that you consider your preferences for body care thoughtfully and carefully. Options include *disposal, cremation, burial,* and *preservation.* This book describes these options in detail, including advantages and disadvantages of each. We urge you to investigate these options *in advance,* so that you understand the methods and costs involved. It will give you peace of mind to know that the choices you've made are *informed* ones — not ones made in haste and when your mind is clouded with grief. Avoiding these decisions or leaving them to somebody else when the time comes only adds to your pain and prolongs your grief. Taking responsibility for the situation lets you prepare yourself for your loss long before your pet dies.

Ask yourself how you want to feel when you look back upon the arrangements you've made. What treasured memories can you make now that will later give you comfort and peace? Even if you know your pet's death is imminent, you can make the remainder of your time together very special. Talk with fellow animal lovers or specialists in pet bereavement, who understand the bond you have with your pet and can help you decide what to do. Embrace the short time you have left with your pet by spending quality time together. Indulge in your favorite activities. Take lots of pictures — and as one pet owner said to us, "When you think you've taken enough, take some more!" Take snapshots, videos, even a professional portrait if you like. Take a clipping of your pet's fur. Preserve a paw print. Save a feather. Find and read some of the excellent books written for grieving pet owners. (See Recommended Readings at the end of this book.)

## Sorting Out Your Own Values and Beliefs

Facing a major loss usually causes us to confront and rethink our basic beliefs about God, religion, death and the afterlife. While some of us turn to God as a source of strength at the time of a beloved animal's serious illness or death, others question the religious faith we grew up with. Some of us may have had no religious upbringing at all, yet still feel abandoned by God or angry with God for letting our pets get sick and die. Not all people respond to loss in the same way, and not all people share the same cultural, religious or spiritual beliefs about death, body care and the afterlife. We all have our own viewpoints on these matters.

Many of us wonder where our animals "go" when they die, whether our pets have souls, or whether we will reunite with our animals in an afterlife. Much has been written by clergy and others on the subject of animals having souls and whether animals go to heaven. Although we cannot resolve this issue for you, we do believe that, like any other tool, religion can be used or abused. Whether your own faith will be a help or a hindrance to you depends on what *you* believe and how you practice your beliefs. After all, religion can be used in healthy, appropriate ways, or it can be abused in unhealthy, inappropriate ways.

As you think about the care of your pet's body after death and consider all the options available to you, keep in mind that *whatever you decide to do with your pet is the right decision, so long as you feel comfortable with it.*

How do you "get comfortable" with this important decision? First, try not to rush into anything (or allow yourself to be rushed into a decision by someone else, no matter how good their intentions.) Otherwise you may do something you'll come to regret later. *You* are the one who must live with the consequences of your decisions. Approach matters when you're calm, and feeling in control of your emotions. Consider your current and future circumstances, including finances and lifestyle. And examine your own beliefs, so that whatever you decide will be consistent with *your* value system.

Many of us haven't even thought through what we believe about our *own* death, let alone that of our companion animals! It's difficult to confront and resolve our own feelings about death, dying, loss and grief. Yet getting in touch with these feelings and clarifying our beliefs will shape how we'll decide to care for our pets after death, as well as how we'll feel about our decisions later.

If you believe that animals have spirits or souls, what happens to your pet's body after death may not be as important to you as the quality of life you gave your animal beforehand. You may even think that resources set aside for after-death body care would be better spent on animals already living and in need of loving care.

On the other hand, you may believe that your pet's body should be treated with the same dignity and respect accorded any other departed family member, and to do anything less would dishonor your pet's memory.

If your animal is very large, such as a llama or a horse, the difficulty and cost of burial or cremation may be prohibitive, and those harsh realities must be considered also. (One alternative is to cremate or bury only a portion of your animal's body. You may wish to keep the wool from your llama — or save the horseshoes and clip some of the hairs from your horse's mane or tail.)

# Arranging for After Death Care

**Investigating the Options: Key Questions to Ask**

Whatever you decide about after-death care of your pet, make certain that your choices are based on *your* values and beliefs and that they meet *your* emotional needs and financial requirements. Ask yourself these questions:

- What after-death pet care resources are available in my community?
- What is my financial status?
  - Will my situation be the same as it is now when my pet dies?
  - Can I afford the option I prefer?
  - Will I want the same option for any other pets I may have?
- Is home burial prohibited or restricted in my area?
- Is it important to me to have my pet's physical remains near me or with me?
- Will I want my pet's final resting place to be a place that I can visit?
- Do I plan to move at some point in the future?

**Options Available**

**Disposal** of animal bodies is a service offered to pet owners who choose to leave their deceased pet with their veterinarian, animal shelter or humane organization. Some pet cemeteries and pet crematories offer this service as well.

*Method* — In accordance with local, state and federal guidelines, arrangements are made with a third party either for *placement in a landfill* or *rendering*. Bodies of animals to be placed in a landfill are usually discarded together and covered with soil as part of the landfill's routine operations. Animal remains sent to be *rendered* are boiled down to fat and other by-products, which can be recycled into many other products, including animal foods, soap, makeup, toiletries, kitty litter and fertilizer. (It should be noted that, while these methods may seem callous, the options available to veterinarians, shelters and businesses for animal disposal are becoming more limited and restricted. In an earlier era, there were far fewer pets in this country, and a lot more private land was available for burial of animals. We also weren't as concerned with pollution, protection and preservation of the environment as we are today.)

*Advantages* — For some pet owners, letting someone else handle all the details is the most acceptable approach, and they are not concerned with how their animal's body is disposed of after death. Although there is a cost involved, disposal is still less costly than most other options. Some owners, particularly those with very large animals such as horses and llamas, may see this as a sensible way to return their animals' bodies to the earth, or to reuse or recycle their animals' bodies after death.

*Disadvantages* — While there are specific rules and regulations governing the disposal of human remains, most states have no such laws applying to the disposal of pet animals. Land-fills can be privately or publicly owned and operated, and a separate area for disposal of animal remains may be designated, although this is seldom the case. When you leave all the arrangements to your veterinarian, local animal shelter or private business, you may have no control over the handling of your pet's remains. As long as that is satisfactory to you, there is no problem with this option. On the other hand, some owners may care very much about what will happen to their pet's body when they leave its disposal to a third party, but they may feel too intimidated or embarrassed to *ask*! You have a right to know where your pet's body will be taken and if your pet's remains will be placed in a landfill or rendered. Ideally you should ask for and receive — preferably *in advance of your pet's death* — descriptions of disposal options and costs, *in writing*, and your expectation that your pet's body be cared for with dignity should be respected.

**Communal Cremation** is a commonly used option, and a sensible one, as long as it's not important to you that your pet is cremated separately, *and* you do not wish to have your pet's cremains returned to you.

*Method* — Together with several other animal bodies, your pet's body is reduced to mineral form by exposure to intense heat. Thus your pet's remains, properly termed "cremains," are co-mingled with those of several other animals. Communal cremains can be discarded, or scattered or buried on the grounds of a pet cemetery, usually in an area set aside for that purpose.

*Advantage* — Cost of communal cremation is relatively low compared with separate cremation.

*Disadvantages* — Since cremains are co-mingled, it will not be possible to separate one pet's cremains from those of another, so you'll never have access to your pet's cremains, no matter how much you may wish to have them later.

**Separate Cremation** is done when the owner wants only the cremains of his or her own pet returned, either to scatter, to bury or to keep.

*Method* — The animal's remains are kept separate from those of other pets in the cremation chamber, as the individual pet's body is returned to its elements through intense heat and evaporation. The process is completed in one or two hours and results in a quantity of ash and fragments of bone, which are processed, reduced, and returned to the owner in a temporary or pre-purchased container or urn. Cremated remains are odorless and can be stored indefinitely, although the amount will vary depending on the pet's overall body structure. Urns (permanent receptacles specially made to hold cremains) are available in a wide variety of styles, shapes, sizes and materials. (See the *Appendix* at the end of this book for further information.)

*Advantages* — You can choose to view your pet prior to the cremation, and you can ask to be present while your pet is cremated. Separate cremation also offers you greater flexibility than any other option. For example, you can:

- Place your pet's cremains in a memorial container that you can take with you wherever you move.

- Display your pet's cremains in a special container or in a special place of honor in your home.

- Help other family members maintain a bond with your pet by dividing the pet's cremains among them.

- Pick a place in the yard or in the country that holds special memories for you and your pet, and bury or scatter the cremains there, as a way of releasing your pet's body and spirit back to the earth and sky.

- Keep your pet's cremains in an urn that is sealed in a niche, then placed in a columbarium (an arrangement of niches, indoors or outdoors) at a pet cemetery or crematory.

Although costs vary, cremation is readily available, and arrangements can be made well in advance.

*Disadvantages* — Separate cremation is more expensive than a communal one. Unfortunately, the only way to make certain that the cremains returned to you belong to your pet is for you to be present while your pet is cremated. Even if you choose not to witness the cremation, you should ask whether it is permitted. Reputable pet crematories will respect your wishes in this matter, and your suspicions should be raised if they don't.

**Here are the questions you should ask:**

- Is the pet crematory a reputable one (well established, with a solid reputation in the community)?

- What services are available, and what are the costs? (Descriptions, fees and contracts should be in writing.)

- Are pre-planning and pre-payment plans available?

- Does the crematory offer separate cremation, and how is that defined?

- Does the crematory permit you to be present during the cremation of your pet?

- Can you tour the facility?

- Will a crematory representative pick up and transport your pet's remains?

- Will the crematory prepare your pet's body for viewing or for a memorial service?

- How will your pet's cremains be returned to you, and in what time frame?

**Communal Burial** is a service offered to veterinarians by some animal shelters and pet cemeteries. Having considered your own values, emotional needs and financial resources, you may conclude that your pet's after-death care does not warrant significant cost or ceremony. Recall that, for some, an animal's body after death is simply an empty shell that has no meaning once the pet's spirit has left it. If that is your belief, you may feel comfortable asking your veterinarian to make arrangements for communal burial of your pet, or you can investigate for yourself which organizations or businesses in your community provide this service.

*Method* — Your pet is buried along with many other animals in a single mass grave at an animal shelter, or on the grounds of a pet cemetery, or at a city landfill. Although landfill grounds may be set aside specifically for the burial of animals, don't assume that is the case. We urge you to check with your veterinarian or animal shelter about the exact nature of communal burial in your community. As with other options, *don't be afraid to ask!*

*Advantage* — Communal burial is one of the least expensive options available.

*Disadvantage* — Because of environmental restrictions and lack of affordable land, communal burial is no longer an option in many parts of the country.

**Home Burial** is an option that appeals to many pet owners, because the animal's final resting place is on the pet owner's property.

*Method* — The animal should be kept in the coolest part of your home until the grave is prepared. Spread a sheet of plastic on the floor, to protect it against body fluids that are normally released after death. Place a blanket or towel over the plastic, then position your pet's body on top, with the head and legs tucked into a sleep-like position. (Positioning is especially important if you'll be placing your pet's body in a casket-like container some time later, because the body will normally stiffen and cool within hours after death.) It is normal for your pet's eyes and mouth to be open, with the tongue slightly protruding.

At this time you can touch, stroke, hold and groom your pet's body as you wish. If you haven't already done so, you may want to take a feather, a paw print, or a clipping of your pet's fur.

Select a grave site that is sufficiently far enough away from water, gas and electrical lines, and deep enough to prevent the escape of odors that could attract other animals (at least three feet down). When you're ready, place your pet's remains — along with a favorite toy, blanket or other special memento you may wish to include — in a thick liner bag, then enclose in a tight-fitting container made of wood, metal or plastic. (Commercially-made caskets for pet burial are available, as are memorial markers for grave sites. See the *Appendix* for further information.)

*Advantages* — For those who live in rural areas or suburban communities that allow it, home burial is a desirable option. The cost is low; the site and the memorial ceremony can be as simple or as elaborate as you choose, and you can visit your pet's grave whenever you wish.

*Disadvantages* — Depending on local ordinances, home burial may be prohibited in your community. We suggest that you call and ask for a copy of the rules and regulations that govern this in your community. If your animal is very large and your property is not, you may face restrictions in a rural area as well. And the day may come when you must sell your property, move away and leave your pet's remains behind.

(Note that, for a fee, some pet cemeteries or crematories will exhume and transport your pet's remains for burial in another location. Similarly, you can arrange with some businesses for the exhumation, cremation and return of your pet's remains. PALS offers such services. See the *Appendix* for more information.)

**Cemetery Burial** is a way of having your pet's body transported, prepared and buried in an individually marked plot. While some may consider this a little eccentric, extravagant or odd, keep in mind that we humans have buried our pets in ceremonial fashion for thousands of years. Taking responsibility for the proper after-death care of your pet is a very positive and desirable approach, and you should feel free to choose this or any other option without embarrassment. Just be aware that, although there are over 600 pet cemeteries throughout the United States, their services are not standardized and can vary widely both in quality and cost. The information that follows will guide you as you explore this option.

*Method* — Working directly with the pet cemetery representative, you can arrange to have your animal's remains picked up from your home or from your veterinarian's office when the time comes. Services offered vary with the provider, but may include a casket, a viewing (that is, seeing your pet before burial), a memorial service, a burial plot or vault, a memorial marker or a monument, and perpetual maintenance of the burial plot. Burial can be in the ground or above the ground, although mausoleum burial (when the pet's casket is sealed in a crypt) is not offered by every pet cemetery. Costs vary considerably, depending on how simple or elaborate your choices are.

*Advantages* — A pet cemetery should offer exactly what a regular cemetery does: the peace of mind that comes with knowing you're paying a fitting tribute to a cherished friend or family member. Your pet's grave site will be well cared for, in a peaceful, quiet setting that you can visit at any time — and the grave will be properly tended even if you move away.

*Disadvantages* —You may still feel as if you're leaving your deceased pet behind if you move. This option may be too costly for you, especially if you have other pets. Few states have laws regulating the operation of pet cemeteries, and adherence to minimum standards is not mandatory. Therefore it falls to you, the consumer, to investigate, compare and evaluate the quality of the services offered by pet cemeteries. Because of the time and effort required, once again we urge you to arm yourself with this information *in advance* of the death of your pet.

A reputable pet cemetery should be willing to give you satisfactory answers to all of your questions — and if that's not what you experience, we suggest you consider going elsewhere.

**Here are some issues to consider:**

- Is the pet cemetery well established, with a solid reputation in the community?

- How long has the pet cemetery been in business?

- Is the land deed-restricted (for use only as a pet cemetery)?

- Is the property dedicated and protected (with an irrevocable trust or perpetual care fund) to ensure that the land will always remain a pet cemetery and the grave sites will always be maintained? At what cost?

- What services are available, and what are the costs? (Descriptions, fees and contracts should be in writing.)

- Are pre-planning and pre-payment plans available?

- Will the pet cemetery representative pick up and transport your pet's body?

- Will the pet cemetery prepare your pet's body for viewing?

- Can you tour the facilities?

- Can you be present at your pet's burial, and view your pet beforehand?

- Are there any restrictions on visiting your pet's grave?

**Preservation** was originally developed for preservation of museum specimens, but now it's available to pet owners as well.

*Method* — Preservation is a specialized form of taxidermy that captures the natural characteristics of the pet. Skilled practitioners of this art create a life-like image which reflects the pet's nature and personality. Cost varies depending on the pet's size and the length of time required to complete the process.

*Advantages* — Some pet owners want their pet's remains close by, but in a manner more realistic than displaying cremains in a container. Preservation produces results that are very lifelike and long-lasting. Although this method of body care will not appeal to everyone, it is an appropriate choice for some, and you certainly should feel free to investigate it if the idea appeals to you. (Pet preservation is one of the services offered by PALS. See the *Appendix* for more information.)

*Disadvantages* — Preservation is not available in all areas of the country, and not all providers are equally skilled in the process. Some people still consider preservation of companion animals shocking, repulsive or morbid, and owners who choose this option should be prepared to deal with such reactions.

# Providing for Pet Care in Case of Your Own Unexpected Absence or Death

How often do we leave our companion animals home alone, never stopping to consider what would happen to *them* if something unexpected happened to *us*?

Circumstances may be such that we're unable to get home to water, feed or take out our pets. What would happen to your pet, for example, in the event that you suddenly become ill or incapacitated, are in an accident, are hospitalized, are placed in a long-term care facility, or die?

Providing for your pets in your absence is an important part of responsible pet ownership, especially if you're elderly or if you live alone.

Here are some ways to provide for your pets should you be unable to get home:

- Place a sticker on your home's front door or window to inform firefighters, police or emergency medical technicians that you have a pet or pets inside. Include the type of pet (cat, dog, bird, etc.), how many, and where the pet(s) can be taken in case of emergency.

- Make certain that at least one of your neighbors knows what you want to do about your pet(s) if something happens to you or you're unable to get home.

- Designate a friend or relative who's willing to become your pet's caretaker in your absence. Be sure this caretaker has access to your home (a key to your house or apartment), knows what type and number of pets you have and their names, and knows your veterinarian's name, address and phone number. (If friends or relatives aren't willing or available, check to see if you can arrange in advance for a local animal shelter to take your pet, along with a donation to cover expenses, until your pet can be placed in another home. If your animal is a particular breed, a breeder or rescue service for that breed may be of help to you.)

- Carry a wallet-sized card with you that lists your pets by type and name, where they are and who should care for them (including name, address and phone number) in case of an emergency. (Such wallet alert cards are available from the Companion Animal Association of Arizona, Inc., P.O. Box 5006, Scottsdale, AZ 85251-5006, Telephone 602-258-3306.)

- Add an amendment (a "codicil") to your will that specifies the arrangements you've made for your pet's comfort and care, and give a copy to your pet's designated caretaker. For further information, including sample will provisions, you can request a copy of the brochure, *Providing For Your Pets in the* Event *of* Your Death *or* Hospitalization, published in January 1996 by The Association of the Bar of the City of New York, Committee on Legal Issues Pertaining to Animals, Office of Communications, 42 West 44th Street, New York, New York 10036-6690, telephone (212) 382-6690.

- Gather all your pet's important papers and send copies to your pet's designated caretaker. Include your pet's type, breed, sex, birth date, description, license number, photograph, certificates of registration and pedigree if any, medical history and record of vaccinations. Add any special instructions such as diet, favorite treats and toys. State what you'd like done with your pet's body after death.

What will happen to your pet if you do not plan for the future? Sadly, in the confusion that accompanies your sudden illness, incapacity, hospitalization or death, your beloved companion could be overlooked or forgotten, or even taken to an animal shelter to be adopted or euthanized. It doesn't have to be that way, if you're willing to plan ahead.

# Meaningful Ways of Memorializing Your Pet

Elaborate funeral arrangements and lasting memorials have been used to honor beloved departed pets for thousands of years. Death ceremonies and rituals play an important part in meeting our social and emotional needs, helping us support one another as we come to terms with the reality of our loss.

To memorialize a pet is to acknowledge and honor the important role your pet played in your life. It helps bring meaning to your loss and draw closure on your grief. As you think about paying tribute to your pet, feel free to summon up your memories — they'll comfort you and help you keep your pet's love and presence in your heart. Think of what was special about your pet. Reminisce with family members or others who knew your pet. Look over old snapshots. Talk about the funny or silly (or annoying!) habits your pet had. Such reflections will help you plan your own unique ceremony of remembrance, and will help you express and work through your grief as well.

Make a special place in your home, yard or workplace that acknowledges and honors your pet's life — a place where you can go (or be) and remember your lost friend. Don't be afraid to be creative. The death of your pet is a natural event and an occasion for the honest expression of your feelings and your values. You can honor your pet's memory in whatever way you find meaningful.

What follows is a list of ideas for memorializing a pet, gleaned from the hundreds of grieving pet owners we've worked with over the years. The ideas are as unique and as varied as the people who invented them. Think of ways you can adapt them and make them your own.

- Have a funeral or memorial service for your pet. Involve the whole family in the planning. Make it as simple or as elaborate as you like and invite whomever you choose, as long as it meets your need to express and share your sorrow, pay tribute to your dead pet and support one another as you say goodbye.

- If you're a writer, *write* — it could be an article, an anecdote, a story, a poem, a song, a letter, an obituary or a eulogy for your pet. If you don't want to write for someone else, keep a private journal and write about your feelings as you journey through your grief.

- Write a farewell letter to your pet as a way of saying an in-depth, thorough good-bye. Say what you are feeling, what you will miss most, what you will always remember with fondness. Say what the relationship gave you and tell how your life will be influenced by having known and loved that pet.

- Share anecdotes and favorite stories about the pet who died. Sometimes others need permission to talk about your dead pet. Let them know you would rather keep the memory of your beloved pet alive than pretend that nothing has changed.

- Decorate a candle and light it in memory of your cherished pet.

- Purchase a book — perhaps a children's book — on coping with the loss of a pet, and donate it to your local library or school. Ask the librarian to place a label inside the front cover inscribed "In memory of (your pet's name)."

- If your pet was a champion, decorate a tree or wreath with all your pet's ribbons or awards, or make a memorial shadow box or scrapbook.

- Save something that belonged to your pet (collar, tags, food and water dishes; bed or blanket; toys; a clipping of fur or baby teeth; a feather; a horseshoe, tail and mane hairs from your horse; the wool from your llama.)

- Carry a feather, a clipping of fur or a portion of your pet's cremains with you in a tiny container or locket.

- Collect all the snapshots of your pet in a memory box, an album or a collage.

- Frame a favorite picture of your pet and display it in a special place. Give a copy as a gift to another grieving family member.

- Encourage grieving children to draw pictures or write stories inspired by their memories of their lost pet.

- Have a professional portrait of your pet painted or drawn by an artist from your favorite photograph.

- Have a favorite picture of your pet imprinted on a watch, mug, stein, T-shirt or sweatshirt.

- Buy a statue or a stuffed animal that reminds you of your pet, and put your pet's collar around its neck.

- If you buried your pet in a cemetery or in a yard you must leave behind because of a move, take a picture of the grave site and keep that in a special place you can visit instead.

- Plant a tree, bush, shrub, garden or flower bed as a permanent growing memorial to your pet. Mark the site with a memorial plaque, marker or statue.

- If you've saved combings or fur clippings from your pet, have them cleaned, spun into yarn, and made into an afghan, garment or rug.

- If you have your pet's cremains, scatter or bury them in your pet's favorite outdoor place, or put them in a potted plant that you can take with you should you move.

- Keep your pet's cremains in a box or an urn that you can display in a special place of honor in your home or office.

- Inscribe a plaque or nameplate with your pet's name, years of birth and death, and whatever else you choose to write in tribute. Put the plaque on a framed photograph or wooden memory box, hang it on the wall, attach it to a garden bench or other piece of furniture, or display it near your pet's grave.

- Contact the Official Star Registry (800-275-9590) or the International Star Registry (800-282-3333) to name a star after your pet. You can choose your constellation, and a star map of that constellation will be sent to you with your pet's star marked on it.

- Participate in the Monday Candle Ceremony, a healing ritual begun on the Internet that, with a simple lighting of candles at the same time all across the country (10 p.m. eastern; 9 p.m. central; 8 p.m. mountain; 7 p.m. Pacific) brings grieving pet owners together in love and in spirit.

- Observe National Pet Memorial Day on the second Sunday in September.

- Memorialize your pet in cyberspace by accessing The Virtual Memorial Page on the Internet at http://www.ourpals.com.

- Make a donation in your pet's honor to a pet grief support service, to your favorite animal charity or organization, to a special service organization or to a research foundation. (The cause of your pet's death may guide you in this choice.)

- Volunteer for work in a pet grief support service, an animal shelter, humane organization, or other "people helping animals/animals helping people" program.

- Become an active member of your local humane society. (Please refer to the *Appendix* for Arizona information.)

- Join or help start a pet grief support helpline, group or service in your community.

# Understanding Loss and Resolving Grief

**The Process of Grieving**

Losing a cherished companion animal is like losing a crucial part of ourselves. We feel cut off from something very precious that gave meaning, purpose and security to our lives. It's as if an essential part of us has also died. Grieving for a pet can be especially difficult when strong attachment to animals is neither accepted nor understood by others, especially by family and friends. Everyone's relationship with a pet differs, even among members of the same family.

Those uncomfortable with the pain of your grief may avoid you or the topic of your loss, denying you the emotional support you so badly need. However well meaning their intent, some people may encourage you to diminish or deny how deep your pain really is, telling you that "it was just an animal," "you can always get another," or "it's time to move on." Your religious beliefs may lead you to conclude that such pain over a dead pet is exaggerated or unjustified.

Yet pain over the loss of a beloved companion animal is as natural as the pain we'd feel over the loss of *any* significant relationship. Our pets offer us a kind of loyalty, devotion and unconditional love that cannot be found in the more complicated relationships we have with relatives, friends and neighbors. Is it any wonder that we feel so devastated when all of that is gone?

By understanding the grief process and how people feel when they're grieving, you will discover that you are *not* "going crazy," that the devastating pain will not last forever, and that there are steps you can take to help yourself get through this difficult time.

## The Experience of Loss

Losing someone you love can arouse a host of emotions, from extreme sadness to a sense of relief when a life that had been full of pain and suffering has come to an end. Each person's experience of loss is different and unique to that individual, and how we express our grief varies from one person to another. Although the course of grief is unpredictable and uneven, we all get through it in ways that are personally meaningful to us. Everyone's grief pattern differs, but over time most people will experience each of the following (in no particular order, sometimes only once, often many times, and maybe several years later.)

*Shock and Disbelief* — Especially if your pet's death was sudden and unexpected, but even if it was anticipated, the initial reaction is one of numbing shock, disbelief, even denial. The magnitude of the loss is too much to take in. It is nature's way of cushioning the blow. While intellectually we may understand that our pet has died, it may take a day or two until we feel the emotional impact of the news. Accepting the reality of your loss is easier if you can see, touch or hold your pet's body as you say good-bye, and if you can talk to someone about the details and circumstances of your pet's death: the when, where and how. The more you talk about the death, the more real it will become for you, and the sooner you can get on with the work of grieving.

*Emotional Release* — When the numbing shock leaves, the pain of loss is felt. Sooner or later reality sets in, and it feels as if you've been hit by a truck. You may be flooded with tears of sorrow, and pain washes over you in waves. Your heart hurts, and you may feel as if it will break.

Your instinct may be to run away or to busy yourself in other matters, but what you need to do is acknowledge your loss, express your grief, and work through your pain. Find someone you can talk to, someone who knew your pet or knew how deeply you were attached to your companion animal.

*Anger* — You'll probably find yourself feeling angry about all sorts of things, and the reasons may vary from one day to the next. You may be angry at your pet for leaving you, or angry at your surviving pet for not being the one who died. You may be angry at the veterinarian for failing to save your pet, or angry at yourself for not doing enough. You may direct your anger at those people who still have their pets, because they aren't suffering as you are. You may be angry at God for letting your pet get sick and die. Sometimes you'll just be angry that the sun is shining and everyone else thinks it's a beautiful day. Consider that, for some of us, feeling angry may be preferable to feeling the hurt and pain of loss. In any case, feeling anger while grieving is *normal*, and it will pass in time. Remember that such feelings are neither good or bad, right or wrong — they just *are*. Try not to judge yourself or censor such feelings when they come up. Instead, simply acknowledge them as *normal*.

Judge yourself not on how you feel but rather on how you *behave*. There are lots of ways to discharge the negative energy that comes with anger without hurting others. You can take time out and count to ten. You can pound a pillow or tear up an old telephone book. You can clean the house; wash the car; take a brisk walk or run around the block; play racquet ball or tennis; chop wood or paddle a canoe. Find someplace private and safe where you can go to cry, yell, or scream at the top of your lungs, and let all your emotions out.

*Guilt* — Grieving pet owners commonly express a feeling of responsibility or remorse for what they did or failed to do for their dying pets. On rare occasions such guilt may be justified (if the owner is grossly negligent or abusive, for example), but in most cases it is not. If your pet was diagnosed with a terminal illness, you may feel guilty for not having noticed symptoms sooner. You may feel guilty about your decision to euthanize your pet, thinking you should have let your pet live longer. On the other hand, you may feel guilty that you didn't euthanize your pet soon enough, thinking you were selfish in your unwillingness to let the animal go. If your pet was critically hurt or killed in an accident, you may feel guilty that you didn't foresee it or prevent it.

Know that guilt is a normal part of grieving. It's only human nature to dwell on the *what ifs* and *if onlys*: "If only I'd done something differently, this never would've happened." Yet it's probably safe to say that, when your pet's accident, illness or death occurred, whatever happened was not *intentional* on your part. You were doing the best you could and, given the information available to you at the time, you were doing what you normally would have done. Harsh as it may seem, consider that even if you *had* done things differently, your pet still could have died in some other way the very next day! Sometimes we act as if we can control the random hazards of existence, even when we know that death is a fact of life.

Healthy guilt allows us to own up to and learn from our mistakes. It gives us a chance to make amends, to do things differently next time, to come to a better understanding of ourselves, to *forgive* ourselves.

Listen to the messages you give yourself (the *should haves, could haves* and *if onlys*), and realize the past is something you can do absolutely nothing about. Have a visit with your lost pet — or have the pet write a letter to you. What would your pet say to you about the guilt and sadness you've been carrying around? Think of all the good things you did in your relationship with your pet and all the loving care you gave. Write those things down, hold onto them and read them when you need to. Or channel your guilt into a worthwhile project. If you've learned a lesson from this loss, you may want to share your newfound knowledge with other pet owners, so that other animals won't meet with the same fate. As soon as you feel ready to do so, it may help to review the medical facts of your pet's case with your veterinarian, to reassure yourself that you did all you possibly could under the circumstances.

*Physical Sensations* — You may feel an emptiness or a hole in the pit of your stomach, a lump in your throat, or tightness in your chest. You may find yourself sighing often, feeling weak or tired, and without any energy. Your mouth may feel dry; your head or stomach may ache. Your sleep pattern may be disturbed by restlessness, nightmares or insomnia. Your eating habits may be altered, causing to you to gain or to lose weight. Most of these sensations are temporary and no cause for alarm. But the stress of grieving can affect your immune system and your physical health, especially if you have a history of health problems. Let your physician know what's happening in your life — and take good care of yourself. Drink lots of water and eat balanced meals that are easy to fix and digest. Use relaxation exercises or tapes to help you get the rest you need. Realize that taking your pet outside for a walk or a romp in the park may have been what stimulated you to get a daily dose of the fresh air and exercise you need so badly for yourself now — then force yourself to get going.

*Depression* — Feeling hopeless and sad after the loss of your beloved companion animal is natural, although the intensity and duration of the feelings will vary from one person to the next. Depression saps your energy, making simple tasks like getting out of bed in the morning, getting dressed and preparing a meal seem overwhelming. Everything seems so pointless. You may feel negative and critical toward everything and everyone. You may prefer to be alone, withdrawing from family and friends. At a time when you need others the most, you may feel too fatigued to reach out for help. Know that others may be finished listening long before you're done with your need to talk. It's not that they don't care about your grief — it may be that they want you to feel better sooner than you're able. It's important at such times to turn to someone you can trust, who will not pass judgment on your attachment to your pet or your reaction to your loss. You need someone who will help you acknowledge and express your pain.

You may find yourself crying at the slightest provocation, and sometimes you'll think the tears will never stop. Let them come. Crying is a healthy way to express and discharge feelings.

Although you may be tempted to turn to medications or to alcohol, it's best to use them sparingly. Because antidepressants take so long to work — about two weeks — they aren't of much use anyway in relieving normal symptoms of grief. Anti-anxiety agents may numb your awareness and inhibit the necessary process of getting in touch with and expressing your feelings of grief. Alcohol is itself a depressant, which only adds to your feelings of sadness and could make you feel even worse.

In our work with grieving pet owners, we have found that thoughts of suicide are not unusual, especially when the person is deeply attached to the pet, when the animal's death is sudden, and when the person lives alone. When an animal is such an integral part of someone's life — in some cases the only friend or family the person had — it can be difficult for that person to imagine life without the cherished pet. There is a vast difference, however, between merely *thinking* about suicide and *acting* upon such thoughts. In grief, thoughts of suicide are usually fleeting, and reflect how desperately we want the pain of loss to end.

How do you know if you're suffering from grief or from clinical depression? It's been said that in grief the *world* looks poor and empty, whereas in depression the *person* feels poor and empty. If after a reasonable period of time you find that the sadness you feel is severe enough to interfere with your ability to function at home or at work, if you feel you are "coming apart" and no longer in control, *if you feel suicidal*, we urge you to seek outside help at once! Depression is a *very* treatable problem — and help and understanding are available. Suicide helplines and emergency community mental health services are available throughout the country, 24 hours a day — and are as close as your telephone book.

*Fear* — Losing someone we love reminds us how fragile and temporary *our* lives really are. Until now, we may not have thought much about how vulnerable *we* are to accidents, terminal illness and death. We tend to think of death as something that happens to other people — or to other people's pets. When it happens to us, it's frightening to discover that we don't have as much control over our lives as we may have thought. You may worry constantly, feel disorganized and forgetful, or find it difficult to concentrate.

If you live alone, without your pet's reassuring presence, you may find yourself afraid of the dark or startled by loud noises. One of the most unsettling (yet very common) experiences in grief is the sensation of seeing, hearing, smelling or touching the lost loved one — days, weeks or months after the death has happened. Sometimes as long as a year after the death of a beloved pet, owners will report sensing the pet in the room or hearing it scratching at the door. They *believe* the animal is there, yet they also know their pet is dead. If you don't expect it, this experience can be very frightening and disorienting. On the other hand, if you know that this is very common and perfectly normal during times of loss, you may find it quite comforting and helpful.

*Association with Past Losses* — If you've undergone a recent loss, or if you've sustained a number of losses in the past, your pet's death may stir up many old feelings and memories. If your pet once belonged to a loved one who has died, you may feel doubly bereft when this pet dies because that precious link is lost. There will be certain milestones in your life, such as holidays and anniversary dates, when your

grief will come flooding back — especially in the first year after the death of your pet. Be aware that the critical times are at the three-month mark, and at the first-year anniversary of the death. There will also be times when your grief hits you when you least expect it, and you'll feel completely caught off guard. Know that these "grief attacks" are normal, and not to be considered setbacks.

You can celebrate certain holidays differently from how you did when your pet was alive, or you can simply decide not to celebrate those holidays at all this year. Some holidays, however, are impossible to ignore. Those are the ones you can meet head-on and prepare for ahead of time. Notify your family and friends in advance what you plan to do, then do as much or as little as you feel comfortable doing. Sometimes it helps to do something so different that the absence of the loved one isn't so obvious — and you can always return to your old traditions next year. This year you are grieving, and if you don't feel up to the expectations of others, change them.

When you're suddenly confronted with a reminder of your deceased pet, you may feel as if you've just been kicked in the stomach. You may start crying uncontrollably. Although such triggers can be frightening, they are very common and they do pass. You need only take a deep breath, acknowledge your grief, and let the tears come. Feelings expressed eventually go away.

*Relief* — You may feel a sense of relief when your pet's life has ended, especially if your pet suffered for any length of time; if you spent vast financial resources on diagnoses and treatments; if the burden of providing care for your sick or dying pet fell upon your shoulders. You have been released from an emotionally exhausting and physically draining experience. Take comfort in knowing that you did all you possibly could have done to care for your beloved pet until the very end.

## Finding the Help You Need

*Allowing for Individual Differences in Grieving* — The way we grieve is as individual as we are, and failure to understand and accept our different ways can lead to hurt feelings and conflict among family members. In general, men grieve differently from women, and children grieve differently from adults. If there are other pets in the household, they may be grieving too. Yet everyone's task is the same: to come to terms with the loss.

Men in our culture have been socialized to believe that they must stay in control, act strong and keep their emotions in check. They are not supposed to cry, be afraid or ask for help. When there's a crisis, they're supposed to be strong for the rest of the family. They may cut off conversations that seem to them too emotional. They may reject offers of support or seem angry if encouraged to share their feelings. Many men will grieve in silence and alone. Behavior that seems inappropriate to others may be a man's way of avoiding feelings or displaying his emotions publicly. A man may seem more angry than sad at the death of his companion animal — but he's probably just angry at the situation, and anger is the only way he knows to express his grief. Accustomed to taking charge and being in control, a man may prefer *doing* something in his grief rather than allowing himself to *feel*.

**Women,** on the other hand, have been socialized to be nurturing, empathic and caring. Because so often a woman is the principal care giver for animals in the household, it is she who will feel not only the loss of her dear animal companion, but also the loss of those daily rituals and routines that she and the pet shared. Women in our culture get caught in a double bind: although expected to be expressive and emotional, all too often they are criticized as being *too* sentimental or sensitive. When a woman is grieving, she needs to talk with someone who's comfortable with strong emotions, and who is patient enough to let her discuss her loss *repeatedly*.

**Children** grieve every bit as deeply as adults do when their pets die, although they express grief differently from their parents. Their response to death depends on the knowledge and the skills available to them at the time of the loss. More than anything else, children need their parents to be *honest* with them. They need accurate, factual information; freedom to ask questions and express their feelings; inclusion in decisions, discussions and family commemorative rituals; stable, consistent attention from their caretakers; and time to explore and come to terms with the meaning of their loss.

(Note: For a thorough discussion of children's attachment to their pets and the significance of their loss, we refer you to *Children and Pet Loss: A Guide for Helping*, by Marty Tousley. See *Recommended Reading for Adults and Children* at the end of this book.)

**Other Pets** in the household may not understand what has happened to their companion, but they almost certainly will sense that something's wrong. Pets who've grown up together can be just as attached to each other as we are to them. The surviving pet will exhibit behaviors that are unique to that individual, ranging from indifferent to extreme. The pet may pace or anxiously search each room of your home; refuse to eat or drink; act listless and curl up in a corner; whimper or howl. A pet who was submissive and aloof before may become affectionate and cuddly, whereas another who was loving and attentive may now act hostile and rejecting. Hard as it may be, try offering the surviving pet some extra attention and affection, for you are not the only one experiencing the pain of loss. At first, it may help to leave home with your television, radio or stereo playing softly in the background — and try not to leave the pet alone for long periods of time. Make a fuss over the pet when you do come home, and spend some extra time playing, walking or running together. Remember that you *both* are grieving, and you both will adjust in time.

**Looking First to Those Around You** —The more support and understanding you have around you, the better you will cope with your grief and the sooner you will come to terms with your loss. Not everyone will be sensitive to your needs, especially if they've never loved and lost a very special pet, and if they don't understand the function and importance of grieving. You may encounter relatives, friends or co-workers who unintentionally minimize your loss or, not wanting to see you hurt, discourage you from expressing your grief.

Many grieving people make the mistake of holding their feelings in, giving others the impression that they don't *want* to talk about their loss. Sometimes we need to take the lead in giving those around us permission to talk about our dead pet! By reminiscing and talking openly about how much your pet meant to you, you're letting others know they don't need to protect you by acting as if nothing's happened. If there are youngsters in your life, know that verbalizing, feeling and showing your pain in front of children teaches them that grieving for a lost loved one is acceptable and appropriate.

*Exploring Resources in Your Community* — As public awareness of pet loss spreads, so does the availability of help for bereaved pet owners in the community. For example, The Companion Animal Association of Arizona offers free of charge its **Pet Grief Support Service** (602-995-5885), which provides a 24 hour-a-day telephone helpline; support group meetings; information, literature and reading lists on pet loss; and referrals to appropriate resources. (Although there is no charge for this service, be aware that long distance calls will be returned collect.) The Service is operated entirely by trained volunteers who themselves have suffered the loss of a pet. Ongoing assistance is provided by a certified mental health professional who specializes in pet loss and bereavement, and by a veterinarian affiliated with the Arizona Veterinary Medical Association.

Ask a **pet crematory** or **cemetery representative,** your local **humane society,** your **veterinarian** or your **pet grooming specialist** if they know of any pet loss services in your community — or even if they know of any recently bereaved clients who may be willing to talk with you. Visit your **public library,** local **bookstore** or **pet supply store** and ask for information and literature on pet loss and bereavement. (See the list of recommended readings for adults and children at the end of this book.) Look for pet loss services advertised in your *Yellow Pages* or local **newspaper,** or posted on **bulletin boards** in your grocery store, library, church or school.

If you have a **computer** and access to the **Internet,** there are all sorts of places to go that offer information and support to people who are grieving the loss of a cherished pet. While "surfing the net" is not for everyone, it's clear that there are many, many people across the country who've found their computers helpful in coping with the painful emotions associated with losing a special pet, and through this medium they want to help others as well. (See the *Appendix* at the end of this book for further information.)

**Telephone helplines** are springing up everywhere, some operating 24 hours a day, staffed by compassionate, understanding listeners who have loved and lost their own dear pets and are ready to help others cope with losing theirs.

**Support groups** are not to be confused with group therapy. Their purpose is to lend support to those who have lost or are anticipating the loss of a companion animal. They are *not* about changing your values, your personality or the way you think about things. A well-run support group offers a safe, structured environment in which you can learn about the grieving process, express and work through your feelings of loss, and recognize that your painful experiences are shared by others in the group.

Self-help support groups (facilitated by volunteers who themselves have lost a pet, worked through their grief and are now committed to helping others move through the grief process) can be very effective. Ideally, however, the facilitators will be assisted by a mental health professional and a veterinarian, both of whom have experienced their own pet loss. The **mental health professional** has a strong background and experience in grief education and therapy; understands group dynamics and group process; can provide structure and "ground rules" for the group; and knows how to address the more complicated issues of loss that may come up (anger or thoughts of suicide, for example). The **veterinarian's** contribution is invaluable in helping grieving owners deal with their anger and their guilt. Owners become better consumers of veterinary care when they're encouraged by a veterinarian in a support group to return to their own vet to get answers to whatever questions may be lingering about their pet's illness or cause of death. Grieving owners need to know that they did all they could for their dear pets, and only a veterinarian has the professional medical expertise to offer that level of reassurance. Not all pet loss support groups offer the regular assistance of a pet bereavement counselor and a veterinarian, and you may wish to ask about this as you investigate pet grief support resources in your community.

**Pet Bereavement Counselors** are counselors or therapists who specialize in helping people who are anticipating or coping with the loss of a beloved companion animal. They have education and training not only in loss and bereavement in general, but in **pet loss and bereavement** in particular. They understand attachment and loss as it pertains to the human-animal bond, and their focus is on helping to heal the pain that's felt when that bond is broken. Therapists without this understanding may misinterpret the strength of your attachment to your companion animal and the depth of your grief over its death.

Organizations such as the Companion Animal Association of Arizona and the Delta Society maintain directories of individuals and organizations specializing in pet loss throughout the country, and update them yearly. Listings are also posted regularly on the World Wide Web. (See the *Appendix* for information on contacting these resources.)

## Resolving Your Grief

*Adjusting to Life Without Your Pet* — Gradually, over a three to six month period, you will find yourself adjusting to your loss. You may notice your focus shifting, from *why* this death happened to *how* you can grow through this experience to become a stronger person. Slowly but surely you will find the good days outnumbering the bad, and the spontaneous memories that come up for you will be of happy times, not sad ones. You will come to recognize your loss as real and permanent.

*Forming New Attachments* — In the healthy course of grieving, there comes a time when you feel ready to let go. You will have found a suitable place in your heart for your lost pet, which frees you to go on living effectively in this world. Although you may begin to feel the need for a pet in your life again, you may also fear that to get another animal would dishonor your dead pet's memory. You may feel as if no other animal could take your lost pet's place. We caution you to avoid the risk of jumping too quickly into a relationship with another animal before your grief is resolved. Make sure you've finished grieving your lost pet — that you've identified, expressed and worked through all your pain — so that you are free to appreciate your new pet for itself, and not as a replacement for the one you've lost.

# Helping a Friend Who's Hurting from Loss of a Pet

When someone we love loses a special companion animal, we may not be sure what we can do to help. If anything, we feel help*less*, since we know there's nothing we can do to bring the pet back. We can't take away the pain of the loss. We have no answer to the question, "Why?"

Sometimes another person's loss reminds us of our own past losses — or of ones we ourselves eventually must face. If we've never been as strongly attached to a pet as our friend or family member was, we may not consider the loss as significant as it really was to *them*. If we've yet to experience the loss of a special friend or loved one, human or otherwise, we may not be familiar with how painful such grief can be. And some of us were raised in families that didn't express feelings openly, so we never learned how to comfort others.

Sadly, for fear of saying or doing the wrong thing, many of us shy away from the person who's grieving, or we never go beyond saying "I'm sorry." What else can we do to help a friend who's hurting when a cherished pet is lost?

## What You Can Do to Help

*Just Be There* — You don't have to say anything. Your presence says more than any words can say. If it's appropriate, a hug or pat on the shoulder conveys what words cannot.

*Listen Actively* — Pay close attention. Ask about the facts, and expect to hear the same story over and over again. Repeating is helpful for the griever and acts as a pain-reliever. Let silences and crying happen. Offer suggestions rather than advice. If something similar has happened to you, share — but don't *compare* — your experience, and do so only if asked. Keep the focus on your friend's grief, not your own.

*Accept Strong Feelings* — Strong feelings like anger, guilt and sadness are common and appropriate in grief. Know that feelings expressed go away, while those that are "stuffed" will fester and boil over eventually. Accept whatever you hear, and hold your friend's feelings in confidence.

*Offer Help That's Specific* — Asking for help is difficult for one who's grieving. Rather than saying, "Let me know if there's anything I can do," explain what you're willing to do and ask if it's acceptable. You might offer to go with your friend to pick up the pet's body or cremains, for example, or you could help dig the grave or plan a memorial.

*Extend Condolences and Inform Others of the Loss* — A card, note or letter expressing sympathy or sorrow over the loss of a pet doesn't require an answer; it can be re-read many times, and it can bring great comfort for weeks, months, even years afterward. Inform mutual friends about the loss and together find ways to honor the lost pet's memory (e.g. making a donation to a pet grief support service or a favorite animal charity or organization; purchasing an urn or memorial marker.)

*Gently Suggest Outside Support if Needed* — If whatever you have to offer your friend doesn't seem enough, you can say something like this: "As much as I care about you, I'm unable to give you the help you need and deserve." Encourage your friend to contact a pet grief support service helpline or support group, or to seek professional help.

*Be Patient* — Grieving takes time, and there is no specific time-limit for grief. It's an emotional roller-coaster, with all of its ups and downs. There will be good days and bad ones. (Sometimes we want our loved ones to hurry up and feel better so that *we* can feel more comfortable in their presence.)

## What Doesn't Help

*Answering Spiritual Questions* — Losing a loved one usually leads us to question why God lets bad things happen to good people. Don't feel as if you have to supply the answer. Far better to let your friend find his or her own answers to such spiritual questions. Instead, you can honestly say, "So many things in life cannot be explained, and I guess this is one of them."

*Surprising Someone With a New Pet.* Your friend needs to finish with the loss of this pet before expending energy on another. And for some, getting a new pet too soon would seem disloyal to the lost pet.

*Offering Platitudes and Clichés* — These are the thoughtless, hurtful, trivializing comments we've all endured at one time or another:

- "It was only a dog (cat)."
- "You can always get another."
- "I know exactly how you feel."
- "You'll get over it in time."

*Expecting Gratitude for Your Efforts* — A person who's in pain is focused inward, self-absorbed and has little room for gratitude. When you offer help, be sure that it is wanted, and don't feel hurt or rejected if it's not.

*Avoiding the Topic* — We may think that not talking about another's significant loss is a way of protecting him or her from painful memories. Consider that a grieving person is thinking about very little else anyway, and to avoid the topic is to talk about everything but what really matters to the grieving person! To be sure, memories stir up strong feelings, but they aren't necessarily painful ones.

Being present for someone who's grieving is one of the most generous, compassionate gifts we can offer. When we acknowledge another's loss with comfort, support and understanding, we feel connected in a very special way — and we come to know ourselves a whole lot better as well.

# When is Grieving Finished?

To ask when grieving is finished is to ask how high is up. It's finished when it's finished, and it may take anywhere from a few weeks to four full seasons of a year or more. It is completed when all the pain has been worked through, and because everyone's experience of loss is different, it's impossible to set certain completion dates. While the pain of loss diminishes in intensity, it's never completely gone. We'll never return to a pre-grief state. When we've sustained the loss of a love, we will never be the same.

Perhaps the best thing we can do for ourselves and for the cherished pets we have loved and lost is to keep their memories alive in our hearts and live a good life in their honor. Remember that the love we have for our pets is stronger than death because, even though we miss them terribly, we will love them forever.

Losing a cherished animal can remind us not only how fragile and temporary life is, but also how important it is to appreciate what we *do* have: life, health, family, friends and loved ones (furry, feathered, finned and otherwise). A successful journey through grief leaves us with greater emotional strength and self reliance, and a greater awareness of what really matters in life. Take heart in knowing that the day *will* come when you can think of your lost pet without the wrenching pain and tears. You will feel yourself open to love and intimacy in your relationships with others, and you'll be willing to risk loving and losing and letting go again.

That's the way it goes when we live our lives to the fullest. We love. We lose. We learn. We let go.

And then the day finally comes when we're strong enough to risk doing it all again.

# Recommended Reading for Adults and Children

Listed below are a few of the many excellent books that can help you understand and cope with the pain and turmoil of losing your pet. You can ask for them at your local library, bookstore or pet supply center, or you can contact the publisher directly.

*When Your Pet Dies: Dealing with Your Grief and Helping Your Children Cope,* by Christine Adamec; Berkley Books, 1996 (The Berkley Publishing Group, 200 Madison Avenue, New York, NY 10016).

*Coping with Sorrow on the Loss of Your Pet* (2nd ed.), by Moira Anderson Allen; Alpine Publications, Inc., 1996 (Alpine Publications, 225 S. Madison Ave., Loveland, CO 80537).

*The Fall of Freddie the Leaf: A Story of Life for All Ages,* by Leo Buscaglia; Slack, 1982 (Slack, Inc., 6900 Grove Road, Thorofare, NJ 08086).

*How to Survive the Loss of a Love* (2nd ed.), by Melba Colgrove, Harold Bloomfield and Peter McWilliams; Prelude Press, 1991 (Prelude Press, 8159 Santa Monica Blvd., Los Angeles, CA 90046).

*Life After Loss* (2nd ed.), by Bob Deits; Fisher Books, 1992 (Fisher Books, P.O. Box 38040, Tucson, AZ 85740-8040. Telephone: 602-292-9080).

**Lifetimes: The Beautiful Way to Explain Death to Children,** by Brian Mellonie and Robert Ingpen; Bantam Books, 1983 (Bantam Books, Inc., 1540 Broadway, New York, NY 10036).

*Children and Pet Loss: A Guide for Helping,* by Marty Tousley, RN; CAAA, 1996 (Companion Animal Association of Arizona, Inc., P.O. Box 5006, Scottsdale, AZ 85261-5006. Telephone: 602-258-3306).

# *Appendix*

*For further information on pet loss and bereavement:*

The Companion Animal Association
of Arizona, Inc.
**Pet Grief Support Service and Helpline**
P.O. Box 5006, Scottsdale, AZ 85251-5006,
(602) 995-5885, Internet site: http://
www.goodnet.com/~ej18026/caaa1.html

**The Delta Society**
P.O. Box 1080, Renton, WA 98057-9906
(206) 226-7357    Fax (206) 235-1076
E-mail: deltasociety@cis.compuserve.com
Internet site: http://petsforum.com/
deltasociety/

**Pet Loss Foundation**
1312 French Road, Suite A-23,
Depew, NY 14043

**The IAMS Company**
Pet Loss Support Line
(916) 752-4200

*For further information about pet cemeteries, pet
crematories and pet preservation:*

Katherine Heuerman
**PALS**
3629 N. 40th Avenue, Phoenix, Arizona 85019
(602) 455-6677    Fax (602) 455-9252
E-mail: Katherine@ourpals.com
Internet site: http://www.ourpals.com

International Association of Pet Cemeteries
5055 Route 11, Ellenburg Depot, NY 12935
(518) 594-3000

National Association of Pet Funeral Directors
210 Andersontown Road, Mechanicsburg, PA
17055, (888) 422-1745

Accredited Pet Cemeteries Society
139 West Rush Road, West Rush, NY 14543,
(716) 533-1685

*For information about pet memorial products (urns, caskets, markers):*

Katherine Heuerman
PALS
3629 N. 40th Avenue, Phoenix, Arizona 85019
(602) 455-6677    Fax: (602) 455-9252
E-mail: Products@ourpals.com
Internet site: http://www.ourpals.com

*For comfort and support for pet loss on the Internet:*

Prodigy
The support group is located on PETS BB,
DOGS topic, PETS GO TO HEAVEN subject.
Contact: Ed Williams FYWM31A
(ywm31@prodigy.com)

CompuServe
The support group is located on The Time-
Warner Dogs and Cats Forum (GO TWPETS) in
the SAYING GOODBYE Section. Contact:
Marion Hale 75547.1107@compuserve.com.

### America Online

Use keyword PETCARE in the Animals and Society topic of the PetCare Forum. Contact: Cazoo (cazoo@aol.com)

### GEnie
Type PETS or M295;1 at any prompt.

### Microsoft Network
Support is located in Pets, PetsForum, The Melting Pot.

### World Wide Web
If you're anticipating or grieving the loss of a beloved companion animal, contact the Our Pals homepage at http://www.ourpals.com, for support, assistance and information. Here you'll find "Marty's Pet Loss Column," "The Virtual Memorial Page," "About Our Pals," and "Memorial Products and Services."

Contact the Companion Animal Association of Arizona at http://www.goodnet.com/~ej18026/caaa1.html to learn more about its Pet Grief Support Service, which offers a 24 hour-a-day telephone helpline, support group meetings, information, literature and reading lists on pet loss, and referral to appropriate resources.

Contact the Pets Grief Support Page and Monday Night Candle Ceremony at http://ourworld.compuserve.com/homepages/edwilliams/ for helpful information and links to many other helpful and comforting sites.

Contact the Lightning Strike Pet-Loss Support Page at http://www.netwalk.com/%7Ecopydoc/ pet-loss.html for "lightning fast" comfort, assistance and support.

Use http://www.cyberspy.com/%7Ewebster/ death.html to find the WEBster, an enormous listing of resources on death, dying and grief. To find PETS OR ANIMAL LOSS, scroll down the page to the Master Index and click on Pets or Animal Loss.

*For information about membership in the Arizona Humane Society:*

**AHS Membership Department**
9226 N. 13th Avenue, Phoenix, Arizona 85021
(602) 943-7655

# Index

## A

Accidental death of a pet, 55
Afghan from pet hair or wool, 48
After-death pet care, advance
  preparation for, 1, 15, 43
  choices in, 29
  costs of, 29, 30, 32–39
  options available, 29–40
  resources for, 29
  responsibility for, 15
Afterlife, belief in, 25
Alcohol, effects of, 57
Anecdotes, sharing of, 47
Anger, handling feelings of, 54
Animal charity, donations to, 50
Anniversary dates and grief, 59
Anti-anxiety agents and grief, 57
Anticipatory grieving, 17
Antidepressants, effectiveness
  of, 57
Associating with past losses, 59
Attachment to pets, strength
  of, 7, 68. See also Detachment
  from lost pet
Awards, displaying pet's, 47

## B

Basic beliefs, relevance of, 25
Body care, arrangements for, 15
  home burial and, 35–37
  positioning after death, 35
Book, donation of, 47

Burial of pet's remains, as an
  option, 24
  at home, 35–37
  communal, 34
  exhumation and, 37
  in pet cemetery, 37–39
  in city landfill, 30, 31, 35
  in cemetery plot, 37
  in rural setting, 36
  in suburban setting, 36
  partial burial and, 27
  viewing pet prior to, 37

## C

Candle Ceremony, Monday, 49
Caskets, pet, 36, 78
Cemetery, pet, 37–39
Children, grief and, 62–63
Clinical depression, 56–58
Clippings, saving, 20, 27, 36,
  47, 48
Columbarium, 33
Community mental health
  services, 58
Companion Animal Association
  of Arizona, Inc., 42, 64, 77, 79
Control over life events, 59
Cremains, burial of, 33, 48
  co-mingling of, 31
  definition of, 31
  memorial containers for, 33
  scattering of, 32, 33, 48